LAURA ASHLEY

·DECORATES·
A LONDON HOUSE

Text & Research by
Jane Clifford

Photography by
Arabella Campbell-
McNair-Wilson

CONTENTS

By the same author: A House in the Cotswolds —
The History and Decor of a 17th century English Home (Laura Ashley)

© LAURA ASHLEY LIMITED 1985   ISBN 0-950-89131-2

Printed in Great Britain by Studio Press Limited, Birmingham.

INTRODUCTION

In a sermon of Baldwin Brown's in *'Young Men and Maidens. A Pastoral for the Times'* published in London in 1871, women were urged to remember the need of 'world-weary men' and therefore 'to pray, think and strive to make home something like a bright, serene, restful, joyful work of heaven in an unheavenly world.' Although the language seems rather exaggerated today, the idea of home as a haven from mundane reality has come full circle. Witness the recent spate of new books and magazines on interior decoration and home improvements. People are spending more than ever on decorating their houses and the Englishman's home has become even more his castle. Nostalgia for the past is combined with the desire for increased comfort in the home as a bastion against the horrors of the world outside.

The Victorian era itself evinced increasingly widespread comfort in homes, with the introduction of hot-air heating, gas, and later electric lighting, running hot and cold water, bathrooms and flushing lavatories coming into general use. It is not surprising that the charms of home should have been extolled in the music hall song 'Home, Sweet Home.'

The nineteenth century saw the unprecedented development of domestic urban architecture. Rows of terrace houses from London to Manchester, from Plymouth to Hull provide, even today, a substantial part of our housing needs. During the intervening years, developers have converted them into flats; builders have 'modernised' them, tearing out fireplaces, shutters, doors, plaster mouldings and tiled floors, anything in fact that made them look 'old' fashioned. At last the tide has turned and people, realising that much of the charm lies in their original architectural details and fittings, are conserving and restoring them to something of their former glory.

Laura Ashley Ltd. has taken a house, built in 1862, which had fallen seriously into disrepair and had been crudely converted into flats, with no bathrooms. All of its original fireplaces, tiles and panelled doors had been removed and it was ravaged by dry rot. It has now been returned to something much more like its original appearance and condition, with certain modifications. The missing plaster mouldings, panelled doors and fireplaces have been replaced, and to complete the authentic appearance, Laura Ashley Ltd. has produced a range of wallpapers, textiles, and a carpet, all copied faithfully from originals in museums and houses in England dating from pre-1862 and it is now furnished in period.

The decoration and arrangement of furniture has been completed with the aid of contemporary water-colours, prints and photographs of interiors of the smaller villa and town house. An attempt has been made to explain a little of the philosophy behind Victorian decoration, with detailed descriptions from Victorian books on architecture, interior decoration, etiquette and life.

The change from the regimented formality and sparseness of 18th century interior decoration, to the comfort combined with opulence of the 19th century, can be attributed in part to the increased importance attached to the Family, and the man's change in his attitude towards it and his home. Walter Houghton in *'The Victorian Frame of Mind 1830-1870'* quotes the writings of J.S.Mill in *'The Subjection of Women 1869'*. 'The association of men with women in daily life is much closer and more complete than it ever was before. Man's life is more domestic. Formerly, their pleasures and chosen occupations were among men and in men's company: their wives had but a fragment of their lives. At the present time the progress of civilisation and the turn of opinion against the rough amusements and convivial excesses which formerly occupied most men in their hours of relaxation – together with (it must be said) the improved tone of modern feeling as to the reciprocity of duty which binds the husband towards the wife – have thrown the man very much more upon the home and its inmates, for his personal and social pleasures.' Houghton himself wrote 'At the centre of Victorian life is the family. Since women have always been concerned with the home, its special development in the Victorian period must be attributed to a re-orientation of the masculine attitude.'

Many of the prerequisites laid down by the Victorian architects and designers for making a comfortable family house, can be seen from this book to be as relevant today as they were then. With the aid of photographs of drawings and water-colours, and contemporary descriptions, from which the ideas have been culled, together with 'before and after' photographs of the Laura Ashley house, this book illustrates how a sad, degraded building was restored to something of its former appearance, combining quasi-authentic atmosphere with convenience.

HISTORY
OF · THE · HOUSE

The house is situated near Kensington High Street and Cromwell Road in west London, not far from Holland Park and Kensington Palace.

With the help of the Survey of London, (Greater London Council), and the Royal Borough of Kensington and Chelsea local history library, it has been established that the original building lessee for this house, along with two others, was George Butt, Builder, described of 23 Camden Street, Kensington, who on 4th June 1862, took a lease of the house, which was said to be in course of erection. The lease, for 99 years from 25th March 1862, was granted by Edward Thomas Goldingham of Grimley, Worcestershire, gentleman, who may have been a solicitor and who held the freehold in trust for Dr. Marris Wilson, M.D. of Upper Charlotte Street, and Mrs Ann Brown of Cheltenham, a widow. Another party to the lease to Butt was George Noakes, a local builder who may have been 'off-loading' some of a previous commitment to build in this area. The house has been first identified, though unoccupied, in the rate books in 1863. Two months after his lease Butt mortgaged it to a John Neate of Orchard Street, Portman Square.

The building development of this estate had begun in about 1851, when the freeholder was a banker, James Rhodes of Hackney. The layout of the street pattern seems to have been the work of the surveyor, Samuel Rhodes of Hammersmith. In 1851-2 Thomas Cundy, the surveyor and architect, was also acting for James Rhodes in dealings with the sewer authorities. This may have been either Thomas Cundy the father or son, sometimes called Thomas Cundy II (1790-1867) and III (b.1820), themselves son and grandson of the celebrated architect Thomas Cundy I (1765-1825). The architectural 'style' of the area seems to have been partly preserved during its completion, after James Rhodes had withdrawn from the scene, but whether Samuel Rhodes or Cundy or someone else drew the elevations and plans of the houses is not known.

This is typical of the sort of development that was taking place in London in the nineteenth century with speculative builders developing small areas consisting of a square or two and a few streets. Part of London's special character comes from these small pockets of uniform developments.

THE · EXTERIOR

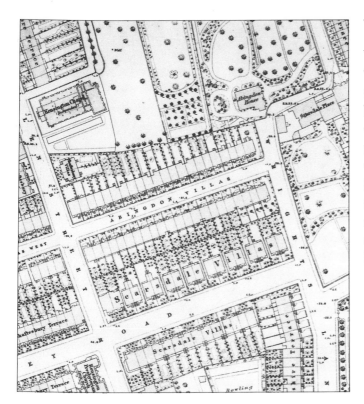

This is a typical London brick and stucco four storey terrace house. It has a three-sided bay window on the basement and ground floor, with pairs of pedimented windows on the first, and shallow arched windows on the second, crowned by a simple flat parapet. The windows are plate glass, large panel sash windows. Scott, a contributor in Loudon's *'Architectural Magazine'* (1835), considered plate glass 'as undivided as possible, one of the most useful and beautiful inventions of our day, and eminently calculated to give cheerfulness to our house'. The back elevation is of plain brick, unadorned.

THE ENTRANCE · HALL

In John Claudius Loudon's *'Encyclopaedia of Cottage, Farm and Villa Architecture'*, first published in 1833, and subsequently reprinted several times by his widow, until the final edition in 1867, the anonymous contributor takes the interior of a house room by room, starting with the entrance hall.

'If the apartments are small and devoid of ornament, I would then substitute for the hall a smaller kind of entrance, with a vaulted roof; and moreover rather gloomy, to increase the general effect of the rooms which open on to it'..... and later 'To assist in furnishing the walls, armour..... together with the horns of stags and other animals taken in the chase might be hung around. To make the hall comfortable it should be warmed with hot air'.

The entrance to this house is approached through a small front garden, and up a short flight of stairs. The dark green front door has had the unsightly frosted glass removed and replaced as originally intended by fielded wooden panels, copying others surviving in the Terrace. Front doors were usually grained or painted black. This door opens onto a long narrow hall, typical of the terraced house. The hall had its original dado rail, but only the torn remnants of a gothic lincrusta (decoratively moulded, heavy duty) paper below it.

Opposite the front door is the staircase. As it was removed during the earlier conversion the bannister has had to be replaced. The bannister uprights were fortunately bought 'off the peg' and match those on the upper landing. The terminal mahogany scroll to the hand rail had to be specially carved, using the original one in the house next door as the pattern. It was essential to replace this accurately as it remains one of the entrance hall's focal points.

The burgundy, navy and sand wallpaper that has been used is a replica of an Owen Jones design, taken from a large leather-bound volume of wallpapers printed by Townsend, Parker & Co., dated 1855 and now in Manchester City Art Galleries.

8

Owen Jones, who was the son of a Welsh furrier, was the author of, amongst other works, *'The Grammar of Ornament'*, first published in 1856. This is universally regarded as one of the classic references on Victorian aesthetics, as well as an important survey of decorative detail from the Stone Age and Ancient Egypt to 19th century Europe. He was the first architect to make a systematic study of Moorish art, as exemplified in the Alhambra in Granada, from which many of his designs derive. Indeed this design is reminiscent of Moorish lattice work. It is completed with a stylised egg and dart border taken from the same volume. The chair rail is picked out in burgundy and the dado and skirting are painted navy blue. Following Loudon's advice the hall is 'rather gloomy', providing an excellent foil to the rooms opening off it.

The staircase well leading down to the basement kitchen and dining room has been painted plain sand and edged with the same Owen Jones border. Wallpaper on the staircase was often confined to the main entrance area and paint was used thereafter in the interests of economy. In this case 'tanking' against rising and penetrating damp ruled out the use of wallpaper for two years. The burgundy stair carpet completes the ensemble.

Originally the stairs would have had a narrower strip of carpet with polished boards showing on either side, possibly clipped by polished brass stair rods, but for modern convenience a fitted carpet has been substituted. The hall is furnished sparsely with a pair of mahogany shell-backed hall chairs flanking a rectangular oak table with a marble top c.1825. It was often customary to stand a silver or plated salver on the hall table, for callers, visiting cards. Above the table is a tall rectangular looking-glass in a gilt wooden frame c.1830. The paterae on the corners echo those ornamenting the apron of the table below. The use of a looking-glass gives the effect of lightening and widening the hall.

The walls of the entrance hall are hung with antlers and a circular bronzed plaster medallion of William Roscoe, M.P. (1753-1831), by the Liverpool sculptor, John Gibson R.A. (1790-1866). Roscoe, a rich 19th century Liverpool banker, was the author of the celebrated two volume book *'The Life of Lorenzo de Medici, called the Magnificent.'* Roscoe was one of the greatest English connoisseurs of Italian 'primitive' gold-backed paintings, and his collection is now in the Walker Art Gallery, Liverpool. The medallion is set in a bog oak and gilt frame, which was probably supplied by another Liverpudlian, George Bullock (fl.1800-1818), Roscoe's cabinet-maker friend. Bullock made an especially patriotic point of using native British woods during the Napoleonic wars.

The hall is lit by a reproduction of a Victorian brass hall lantern. This is fitted for electricity, but the original would almost certainly have been lit by gas. The only window, apart from the fanlight over the front door is on the top landing. It is dressed with a festoon blind of cotton printed to match the wallpaper, with a self frill edged in burgundy.

THE DRAWING·ROOM

Robert Kerr in his *'The Gentleman's House, or how to plan English Residences from the Parsonage to the Palace'* of 1868, writes of the drawing room 'The character to be always aimed at in a drawing room is of especial cheerfulness, refinement and elegance and what is called lightness as opposed to massiveness. The desireableness of end windows in the case of the drawing room ..... The employment of the bay window ..... is of especial service. Indeed it is so general as to need little explanation, certainly no advocacy.'

The drawing room in this house, on the left of the entrance hall is formed by two rooms divided by an arch, and runs the full depth of the house. It might originally have followed the common practise of having large folding doors providing two rooms which, when the owners were entertaining, could be opened to form a single room. From a water-colour of the drawing room of No.3 Chester Place, London, dated 1838, it can be seen that both rooms were decorated with the same wallpaper, and were otherwise arranged as one. The house has the recommended 'end windows', a south-facing 'bay window' at the front and a flat sash window at the back, looking out over the garden. Although both chimney-pieces had been removed the original ceiling cornice of entwined hops remained, though severely damaged by dry rot. J.M.McDonough of Fulham Road, took a mould from what was left and remade in plaster an excellent replica for the whole of the front room.

A simple black marble fireplace of about 1860 has been installed, together with a massive cast iron grate of about 1840, decorated with fruiting vines and a Bacchic procession. Such references to wine suggest that the grate was probably originally intended for a dining room. The relief is taken from a bronze by the French sculptor Claude Michel, called 'Clodion' (1738-1814). It was copied in the later 18th century by Wedgwood in black basaltes and used by Robert Adam (1728-1792) as a door head in Lansdowne House. Such relief sculpture could still be bought from the London Plaster Shops for manufacturers to take casts from them. The flat modern door has been replaced with an old panelled one, and Victorian brass handles and finger plates were found separately and fitted.

Above: The Drawing Room, No.3 Chester Place, London dated 1838. Anon.
Here we can see the formal arrangement of the room, with central circular table covered in a square cloth, hanging lamp above, and heavily fringed and draped curtains.

The anonymous contributor to Loudon's *'Encyclopaedia'* (1833), suggests that there should be in the drawing room 'some contrast between the colour of the walls and the curtains', and he goes on to say that for the ceiling 'a warm fawn colour might be the ground of the whole painting.' The geometric wallpaper in this room is again taken from an Owen Jones design in the book of wallpapers printed by Townsend, Parker & Co., dated 1855. It is in shades of fawn and finished with a border of crimson on fawn recalling the colour of the curtains. The ceiling is painted sandy buff with the cornice and central rose picked out in cream. 'All woodwork should if possible be grained in imitation of some natural wood, not only with a view of having the imitation mistaken for the original, but rather to create an allusion to it and by a diversity of hues and shades to produce a kind of variety and intricacy which affords more pleasure to the eye than a flat shade of colour', (Loudon's *'Architectural Magazine'*, 835). The woodwork here has been grained to imitate the real mahogany, which would have been used in more expensive houses.

Graining was widely used from the 17th-19th century and it was not until the 1890's with the aesthetics of the generation of James McNeil Whistler that white paint became fashionable. It is only very recently that graining has enjoyed a revival. For the drawing room Loudon's contributor envisaged 'fringed curtains with simple draperies in large folds, hung from massive gilded pelmet cornices, with under-curtains of figured muslin with fringe to match the main curtains and upholstery'. In another place he writes 'the curtains I would have of crimson watered silk, without draperies supported by large rods of gilt brass with handsome knobs'.

The Tudor rose design on crimson sateen used here for the curtain and upholstery material was taken from a woven silk textile found on a 19th century settee. It is similar in style to some of Pugin's designs for textiles in the Houses of Parliament and for Windsor Castle. The carved and gilt curtain poles with acanthus finials and the design for the fringed draperies were copied from some supplied to Ashburnham Place in the late 1840's. Behind the curtains are copies of Victorian lace panels made for Laura Ashley from the original punched card jacquards by a Nottingham firm. On the subject of the carpet Loudon's contributor writes 'It should of course be a bordered carpet the colour of the ground shade of fawn; the pattern chiefly shades of crimson'. The carpet used in the drawing room fits this description closely. The two squares of carpet are copied from an early 19th century chenille rug, but in Brussels weave, of the sort much advocated in the mid 19th century. The triple border of laurel, Greek key and foliate scrolls in three shades of crimson on a fawn ground surrounds a central reserve of an interlaced design incorporating gothic quatrefoils.

Loudon's contributor continues: 'The chairs and seats should be without cushions and of a rather plain description so as not to interfere with the splendid effect of the drawing room', and again 'when the chairs of a room are covered with cloth, the principle of unity requires that this cloth and that of the window curtains should be the same, both in kind and colour'. The seating furniture in this room consists of two deep buttoned suites, both French mid nineteenth century which came from a château belonging to the Noailles family in the South of France. One set with turned ebonised legs consists of a settee with two armchairs, one large and one slightly smaller. The latter has a large stool which fits snugly into the front forming a chaise duchesse or a day bed. This set has been covered in the crimson sateen to match the curtains. The other neo-rococo suite with gilt cabriole legs consists of four chairs again in two sizes. These have been covered in a 19th century geometric design similar to the wallpaper. The arrangement of the furniture in the room follows contemporary practise as can be confirmed in the floor plan of a drawing room from designs supplied by Gillow of Lancaster, with a central table in front of the fireplace, and

chairs arranged around it. There were no low coffee tables as are found in most homes today.

Robert Kerr describes such arrangements, 'The furniture in the drawing room: in a small room there will probably be a centre table, perhaps with a chandelier over, the usual chairs and couch, occasional tables, sofa table or writing table, occasional chairs, a chiffonier generally or one or more fancy cabinets, one or more mirrors and a cabinet pianoforte.' The idea of lounging about doing nothing was unfashionable, and the arrangement of furniture was to allow for everyone to be employed either at reading, writing, playing board games, music, or drawing. To this purpose various small easily moveable upright 'scatter' or 'fly' chairs were placed around the room which could be moved up to the table when needed. The three 'scatter' chairs in this room in carved mahogany are similar to designs by W. Smee, i.e. *'Designs for Furniture'* (1850). I quote again from Loudon's *'Encyclopedia'*, 'nothing gives a more dismal effect than an appearance of idleness, everything should be so arranged in the drawing room, as if the persons using the room had been employed in some way or other'.

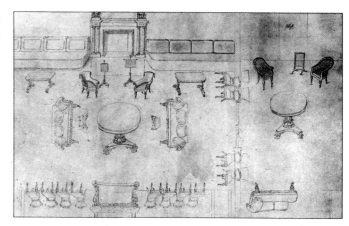

Above: Drawing by Gillow of Lancaster showing the disposition of furniture in a Drawing Room.

The circular table is very often shown covered with a square felt tablecloth like the one on the table in the corner. This one was obviously intended for such a table as it is printed with a circular design in black on red felt. The centre table in this room dating from about 1830 is made of solid rosewood with the top richly inlaid with a brass scrolling frieze running around the top. Its central pedestal rises from a square platform supported on carved paw feet. The method of inlaying brass was similar to that used by A. C. Boulle, cabinet maker to Louis XIV. Sheets of brass and rosewood or mahogany were clamped together, then cut out with a fine saw to the desired design. The two parts 'première-partie' and 'contre-partie' then correspond exactly. From this, two pieces of furniture could be decorated, one with the design in brass and the ground in wood, the other with the design in wood and the ground in brass. This table is of the former type.

The arrangement of objects on and around the chimney piece follows the usual practice of the time, with brass fire irons arranged leaning upright against the jamb, with a brass fender and a hearth rug in front. W.Kent in Loudon's *'Architectural Magazine'* of 1835 writes 'the hearth rug should be of a pattern to agree with the carpet, but bolder, it should be thick, warm and ample in its dimensions.'

A pair of English chinoiserie black lacquer firescreens c.1830 are to the right and left of the fireplace, to protect the ladies faces from the fierce heat of the fire. The lacquered tin coal 'receiver' is painted in simulated burr walnut and brass inlay similar to the table. Such are commonly called 'Pontypool' or 'Usk', although by 1840 there were many manufacturers of this type of tinned ware, particularly in Staffordshire. Over the fireplace is a looking-glass in a gilded wooden frame surmounted by an elaborately carved foliate cresting of about 1845. To the right is a needlework bell pull with a lacquered brass handle. The mantleshelf has a symmetrical arrangement of central clock, pair of cut-glass girandoles with ormolu mounts and a pair of gilt bronze letter racks showing a bear trying to steal honey from a beehive. These inexpensive cast ornaments are often found in America, sometimes as candlesticks with cut-glass lustres. They were probably made in Birmingham, then the 'toy shop of Europe', and exported across the Atlantic in large quantities. W.Kent again suggests 'A clock, a beautiful vase or two, with cut-glass lustrés and a few other choice ornaments may be placed on the chimney shelf.'

By the second half of the 19th century there were various forms of artificial lighting available. Gas lighting was beginning to be introduced into the towns by the 1830's, although it was expensive and gave off an unpleasant odour. Colza and spermaceti oil lamps were still popular throughout most of the 19th century. Colza oil came from the colza seed, and spermaceti from the sperm whale. In this room there is a hanging colza lamp in gilded bronze with a shallow engraved and cut glass dish, as well as a pair of 'Argand' oil lamps, now converted to electricity, made from gilt bronze with Wedgwood drum mounts. Table lamps like this are often found in historic American houses like Boscobel and Sunny Side on the Hudson River, and in fact, this pair was bought in New York which again suggests a flourishing export trade.

Aimé Argand, the Swiss physicist, who died in London in 1803, gave his name to his business of patent oil lamps using either spermaceti or colza oil, with an air burner and a cylindrical wick. The business was registered at 37 Bruton Street. In the 1830's it was taken over by the Bright family of Sheffield platers and became known as 'Bright, late Argand & Co.' His method was used both for hanging lamps as well as table lamps. The oil was poured into an urn-shaped resevoir, or tank, at the top of the lamp, and ran from there along the arm and into the cylindrical wick in the burner.

Argand Lamp

Gothick Side-table

Lacquer Fire-screen

Cut-glass Candle Lustres

Thomas Hopes's 'Household Furniture' - plate 10

Spermaceti and colza oil are so heavy that they functioned most efficiently when draining downwards to the wick.

Candles were, however, still used throughout the 19th century. For a brilliant source of light, cut glass lustres were employed. The prismatic light effect could be enhanced by their being placed in front of a looking-glass. The cutting of the pair here suggests a good London maker, like Parker and Perry, and they date from c.1820. The gilt bronze candlestick with three storks back to back, now wired for electricity, is copied from a massive Roman marble candlestick in the Museo Capitolino in Rome. Two other lamps in the room have been made out of a pair of Limoges mid nineteenth century porcelain vases and wired for electricity. They are enamelled with reservoirs of flowers, on a periwinkle blue and gold ground.

The furniture in this room illustrates the eclecticism of the nineteenth century and the 'Battle of the Styles', with Gothic tracery vying with Egyptian sphinxes and rococo scrolls with classical Greek and Roman motifs. On the left of the fireplace a Gothic writing table, c.1840, in the manner of Augustus Welby Northmore Pugin, the architect of the Houses of Parliament, contrasts with an example of the Regency Egyptian revival, c.1805, in the gilt bronze mount of a standing Egyptian figure on the simulated porphyry upright of a fireplace, which came from Thomas Hope's house in Duchess Street, London. Thomas Hope (1770-1831) was an influential figure in early nineteenth century interior design. He was a Dutch banker, of Scottish ancestry, who designed his own furniture and elaborate interiors, and collected classical vases, Egyptian antiquities and contemporary English sculpture, bronzes and furniture. He made his house open to selected visitors, and published several books including one in 1807 entitled *'Household Furniture and Interior Decoration.'* This neo-Egyptian figure came from the fireplace in the 'Closet or Boudoir', 'fitted up for the reception of a few Egyptian, Hindu and Chinese idols and curiosities.' He too was not averse to mixing styles. He described the rooms briefly opposite each plate.

Of the Boudoir he writes 'The sides of this Lararium are formed of pillars, and the top of laths of bamboo. One end of this tabernacle is open, and displays a mantlepiece in the shape of an Egyptian portico, which by being placed against a background of looking-glass, appears entirely insulated. On the steps of this portico are placed idols and in its surface are inserted bas-reliefs.' On either side of the fireplace are a pair of bronze classical tripods, similar to the one in the other corner of the drawing room here. This particular design derives from a plate in Piranesi's *'Diversi Manieri di addornare i cammini'*, (*Various Ways of Decorating Chimney-pieces*) and prints from this book are in the dining room.

19

An example of the revived Regency Egyptian style is the coromandel clock by Thomas Cole, with gilt bronze mounts of a sphinx and two winged standing figures, which stands in the centre of the chimney-piece. Although this clock is as late as 1860, the mounts were used on a French clock of 1810, showing how moulds for cast ornament were often used years later.

In the classical vein is the mahogany desk c.1825 with two monopodia supports, with a panther head emerging from a single muscular leg, terminating in a claw foot. At the knee joint is a stylised carved acreterion, or Greek honeysuckle, motif. These monopodia were faithfully copied from classical bronze or marble table legs. Thomas Hope was one of the first in England to use them in his designs for modern furniture and subsequently became widely used in the first half of the 19th century.

The ornaments on the top of the desk include a pair of bronze vases by the designer and entrepeneur William Bullock (fl.1800-1840), brother of the cabinet maker George Bullock, already mentioned. William, who dealt in bronzes, plasters and even ceramics, was a colourful figure. He started his career in Liverpool and then moved to London where he was the proprietor of the Egyptian Hall in Piccadilly. This museum, and his earlier museum in Liverpool,

included all kinds of curiosities and acted as a catchpenny for his showroom behind, where the visiting public could buy his bronzes and objets d'art. He owned a silver mine in Mexico and later emigrated to the United States where he had designed an ideal town on the Ohio River, called Hygeia. He died in London in penury. The artist, Benjamin Robert Haydon wrote of him: 'a fine fellow and loved the game of ruin or success – Westminster Abbey or Victory – as well as myself.' Between these two vases is a bronze copy of a classical seated lady 'Agrippina' by Francesco Righetti (1738-1819) after the original marble in the Capitoline Museum, Rome. This was the sort of souvenir that English Grand Tourists brought back from Rome in the late 18th century.

Other sculpture in the drawing room includes a bronze bust of Sir Walter Scott, dated 1830, which is standing on the Thomas Hope pedestal. The bust is by Samuel Joseph (1791-1850), the distinguished Jewish sculptor who carved the celebrated statue of William Wilberforce now in Westminster Abbey. The bust was cast by

Samuel Parker of Argyle Street in the Strand, who in turn was responsible for casting the bronze gates of Marble Arch and many of the fire grates at the Brighton Pavilion. The bust in the window, on another simulated porphyry pedestal, is probably of the great Roman General Scipio Africanus (237-183 BC) and is likely to have been carved in marble at Rome during the late 18th century. To the left, on the floor, stands a large 'Ironstone' neo-classical vase and cover made in Staffordshire in the first quarter of the nineteenth century, with bronzed lion mask handles, the body gaudily decorated in the Japanese taste.

The four-fold screen covered with Islamic crimson and yellow silk richly embroidered with gold and silver thread in Arabic characters echoes the Moorish influence in Owen Jones' interlaced wallpaper border. Near it is a small circular rosewood table c.1860 with scrolling neo-rococo frame rising from a triangular platform base. The top is made out of a section of Derbyshire spa, which looks like a golden brown starfish on a blue-grey ground.

The arrangement of the pictures follows a strictly symmetrical pattern with as near matching pairs creating a balanced architectural hang. Prints were popular and provided a relatively inexpensive alternative to oils. Wherever possible pictures are in their original frames.

To the left of the fireplace is a self-portrait c.1805 of the portrait painter John Opie (1761-1807), known as 'the  Cornish wonder.' When he married Amelia Alderson, a Norwich girl, Opie became a friend of John Crome (1768-1821), the Norwich school landscape painter. The back of this picture has an oil sketch of a distant view of Norwich also by Opie. He was a protégé of Sir Joshua Reynolds, who described him as 'like Caravaggio and Velasquez in one'. Like Reynolds he used bitumen, a tar-based paint, to produce a rich velvety black and brown. Unfortunately, it was not discovered till later that in drying, bitumen shrinks and cockles in a most disfiguring way which cannot be restored.

On the right of the fireplace is a small oil painting by Henry Liverseege (1803-1832), a Manchester artist who specialised in genre and subject pictures. He was much patronised by the local Grosvenor family of Eaton Hall, Chester. Here the subject is from Shakespeare:
'The Ghost of Hamlet's Father appears to his Mother.' Immediately below this is a portrait of Thomas Stothard, R.A. (1755-1834) by Edward Villiers Rippingille (1798-1859). Stothard was one of the greatest book illustrators of his day. With J.M.W. Turner he illustrated Rogers' 'Italy' which elicited from the Countess of Blessington the punning remark that 'the book would have been dished but for the plates.' He was a friend of Constable, Blake and Turner and his portrait was painted by numerous artists. The reason for this may have been that as Librarian of the Royal Academy he was often to be seen sitting in the Academy library. Stothard also designed jasper for Josiah Wedgwood, plate for Messrs. Rundell, Bridge and Rundell, and marble sepulchral monuments. He also painted ambitious fresco cycles like the dome of the Signet Library, Edinburgh, and the staircase at Burghley House. Over the writing table is a half-length

of the portrait of Fénelon, Archbishop of Cambrai, by Joseph Vivien (1657-1734/5) known as the 'French van Dyck.' There are other versions of this portrait in the Louvre and the Altepinakothek, Munich. Fénelon was tutor to Louis XIV's granchildren known as 'The Children of France'. However, he fell out of favour with the king's mistress, Madame de Maintenon, and therefore with the king, and was banished to his archbishopric. He wrote an epic novel called 'Les Aventures de Télémaque' (1699) for the education of his pupil the Duc de Bourgogne, the future Dauphin. Saint-Simon, in his spicy 'Memoires' of the court of Louis XIV, wrote of Fénelon 'He was a tall, lean man, well built with a large nose, eyes that danced and sparkled like a  torrent, and a countenance that, once seen, could never be forgotten ..... It combined gravity with humour, seriousness with gaiety, it expressed in full measure the scholar, the prelate and the great noble. The chief impression made by his face, as by his whole person, was of his discretion, humour, radiance, grace, decency and above all nobility. It required an effort to avert one's gaze. All his portraits are eloquent likenesses; but none catch the delicate harmony so striking in the original, nor the true refinement of all the qualities displayed.' If we are to believe this description of Fénelon this portrait, contrary to what Saint-Simon wrote, seems to have captured many of his characteristics.

On the opposite wall is a group of 18th and 19th century coloured prints that are still mostly in their original frames. Stipple engraving was popular in the late 18th century. The effect resembles a chalk drawing and is obtained by a combination of etching and engraving techniques, by stippling dots over a grounded plate with the point of an etching needle or a special tool (mattoir) giving a chalk grain, or flicking the surface of the plate with the graver. Their revival in popularity in the 1890's to 1920's lead to them being reproduced photographically in large numbers and one has to look carefully to make sure that they are original prints and not a form of more recent photographic reproduction. Today they do not fetch anything like the large prices which they were able to command at the beginning of this century.

The large print in the centre is after Richard Westall's painting (1765-1836) of 'Mary Queen of Scots before the Bishops' and above it hangs 'Love Healed', also by Westall, and to the left 'Arthur and Emmeline' by P.W. Tomkins, (1760-1841), a pupil of Bartolozzi.

Right: Portrait of Thomas Stothard R.A. (1755-1834)
by Edward Villiers Rippingille (1798-1859).

Opposite the fireplace is another symmetrically arranged group consisting of oil paintings, a sculptured relief and old master prints. The central circular painting 'St. Mary Magdalen in Ecstasy', probably Milanese early 17th century, is redolent of the intense religiosity of counter-reformation Italy. Above it is a circular marble roundel double portrait echoing the shape of the picture below. It is signed by Peter Hollins (1800-1866), who trained in London under Sir Francis Chantry, and then returned to Birmingham where he built up a thriving practice. In the 'Annals of the Fine Arts' of 1838 it was said of Hollins that 'Every subject undertaken by him is executed with great care and fidelity and in a most refined taste'. Hollins went to Italy in 1835/6, and exhibited regularly at the Royal Academy.

Below and on the right is Dürer's woodcut of 'Samson and the Lion,' of about 1498. Many of Dürer's original woodblocks survived and continued to be used well after the artist's death. In time the original woodblocks

Above: Joseph William Margetts' 'Corner of a Sitting Room', showing the symmetrical hang of pictures two deep, with wires showing, central table covered with a cloth, and formal arrangement of ornaments on the chimney-piece.

became damaged and worm eaten and in this print white dots in the black printed areas can easily be seen where worm holes have pierced the image, and the black border line is interrupted and missing where the block has been damaged. This example probably dates from as late as the 17th or early 18th century. Flanking it to the

right is a line engraving by Hendrik Goltzius (1558-1617), who worked in Haarlem. Goltzius was one of the chief exponents of courtly Mannerist art in the Netherlands in the late 16th century, and under his influence line engraving reached new pinnacles of perfection. At this time print collecting was at its zenith with amateurs greatly appreciating the works of such earlier masters as Altdorfer, Aldegrever, Dürer, and Lucas van Leyden. In response to this Goltzius executed a series of six 'Masterpieces' illustrating episodes from the *'Life of Christ.'* Each was done in the manner of a different late 15th or early 16th century master and this example, 'The Circumcision', is in the manner of Heinrich Aldegrever (1502-1558). In the crowd on the right hand side can be seen a self portrait of the artist looking out of the picture. Below these two prints are two small oil paintings. 'St. John the Baptist', on oak panel, is by a Flemish contemporary of van Dyck, and the 'Holy Family with Angels' on copper is probably by a French artist working in Italy in the 18th century. There is often more difficulty identifying artists' hands when working on copper, because idiosyncrasies of brushwork are greatly reduced owing to the meticulous standard of finish required.

The style of flower arrangements in the room has been copied from mid 19th century water-colours of interiors. They favoured rounded, bunch-like arrangements, in large urns, and small posies in narrow necked vases. The now fashionable triangular flower arrangement seems a more recent innovation, although its prototype goes back to 17th century Holland.

The effect overall of this room furnished with the aid of contemporary descriptions and images is one of comfort and informality. The room created is both welcoming and relaxing so that, in the Victorian manner, the civilised pastimes of reading, writing, sewing and painting may be properly enjoyed. The placing of chairs and tables allows for conversation and light refreshment, while the disposition of papers, fabrics, pictures and works of art should at once delight the eye and put the owner and his guests at their ease.

Right: Mary Ellen Best. General Norcliffe in his Study at Langton Hall. Note the double and treble symmetrical hang of the paintings, and the use of a border around the walls of the room.

Below: Louisa Paris Drawing Room in Dover Street, London.

THE MORNING · ROOM

Robert Kerr in the *'Gentleman's House'* (1868) writes of the Morning Room: 'In the generality of cases a Morning Room is only required to be of that moderate size ..... the windows may extend down to the floor, whether as sash or casements, the one or more may open on the lawn or flower garden, the latter being perhaps preferable.'

The Morning Room in this house is a small room next to the Drawing Room, which has a door leading into the garden. The only remaining feature that was originally in this room is the Edwardian cast-iron chimney-piece. There is no cornice so a grey and white Laura Ashley trompe l'oeil, stiff leaf foliage border has been used to provide some architectural emphasis. The walls have been painted yellow and varnished with a rag roll finish, achieved by using sand gloss paint over a pale lemon ground, giving a warm sunny atmosphere to a North facing room. The curtains are in an early nineteenth century chintz design of white lilies and carnations on a pale buff scumbled ground. This design has been faithfully reproduced from an original in the Whitworth Art Gallery, Manchester. The pelmet design is taken from Thomas King's *'Upholsterer's Guide'* of 1848 in the Victoria and Albert Museum Library, and is edged with Laura Ashley's dark green 'Nutmeg'. The squab seats on the dark green spoon-back chairs are also in the same material and piped in dark green. These chairs of c.1810, which originally came from Toft Hall, just outside Knutsford in Cheshire, may have been supplied to the Leycester's of Toft by Gillow of Lancaster. These were in very poor condition as they had been relegated to a chicken house but they have now been restored and painted with Laura Ashley dark green paint, following traces of the original paint, and regilded where necessary. Gillow of London and Lancaster was one of the most prolific of furniture making firms in the nineteenth century, supplying good, well made furniture in a variety of styles and woods to the owners of substantial houses. They are one of the best documented manufacturers, as a great number of pieces were stamped with their name, and nearly all their account and pattern books survive in the Westminster Public Library. At the beginning of this century they became Waring and Gillow and expanded into the mass market, to their detriment.

The other furniture in the room includes an early nineteenth century rosewood writing table, and a pair of beech 'scatter' chairs painted in cream with reserves of brilliant copper green to simulate malachite. This decoration picks up the malachite on the inlaid black slate ink stand, the two malachite eggs, and the papier-mâché simulated malachite plate on the table. Besides these are a mother-of-pearl blotter, an Ashbourne marble obelisk, and a pair of mid-nineteenth century gilt brass chamber sticks of vine leaf form. These sticks were used to light your way up to bed.

In the corner of the room is a yellow Siena scagliola (composition marble) column supporting a plaster figure of a female sacrificial figure, after the Antique. Such plaster figures were popular in the eighteenth and early nineteenth centuries and were painted to simulate bronze and marble. This one is by Humphrey Hopper (b.1767-fl.1842), a competent sculptor who also ran a flourishing plaster shop. Not all the models sold under his name were of his invention, or even from his hand. On the other side of the garden door are four waxen plaster portrait medallions, of the great Italian poets Dante, Petrarch, Tasso, and Ariosto, dating from the early 19th century, and still in their original frame.

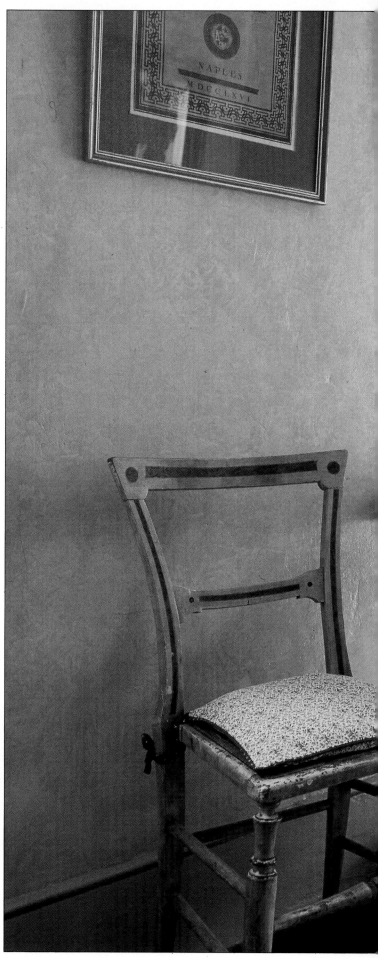

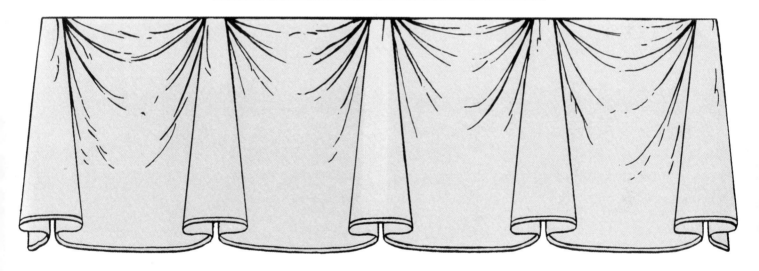

Below: Pelmet design from Thomas King's 'Upholsterer's Guide' of 1848.

The neo-classical flavour of this room is continued in the prints on the walls, which are taken from a lavish three volume work on Sir William Hamilton's *'Collection of Etruscan, Greek and Roman Antiquities'* by d'Hancarville first published c.1767. They are hand-coloured prints of the painted decoration on the Hamilton collection of classical vases, many of which are now in the British Museum. Hamilton, His Majesty's envoy to Naples, was the cuckolded husband of Emma, the love of Nelson.

These prints were copied extensively on pottery by Josiah Wedgwood, as well as by other manufacturers on silver, furniture, wallpaper and printed textiles. On the chimney-piece are placed a pair of double-handled cups and saucers made by Giustiniani of Naples in the 19th century, decorated in black and red with figures copied from such vases. Behind them is an early 19th century looking-glass, painted and grained in simulated rosewood and brass inlay to resemble the table in the drawing room. On the chimney-piece stands a pair of black Ashbourne marble spill vases, inlaid with a spray of flowers in coloured marbles. In front of the fireplace is a brass fender and a mid-19th century black painted wooden coal receiver, decorated with classical motifs in red and gold.

THE
DINING · ROOM
& · KITCHEN

The arrangements of kitchen and dining room are a compromise to modern living as the house must, primarily, be a space for living in and not a museum. For this reason the two main rooms in the basement have been knocked together. At the divide between the two former rooms, curtains have been hung, which can be drawn together to hide the kitchen (when eating), and reduce the smell of cooking. The kitchen is in the smaller back section next to the garden and its original sash window has been replaced by French windows opening onto the garden. The whole of the basement has been tiled with russet coloured tiles. A large oriental design carpet has been placed on top of them in the dining room.

The fireplaces had been removed so a simple early nineteenth century white marble surround has been installed, together with a most unusual grate. It was cast at Coalbrookdale, Shropshire, with a shallow relief elevation of the first Iron Bridge at Coalbrookdale, which was opened in 1781.

There was no ceiling cornice in the room so a rope paper border has been introduced, which is echoed in the rope form of the black and gold carved wood looking-glass over the chimney-piece. The curtains are also edged with the same rope border, in chintz, and the walls are painted sand with smoke blue paintwork and cream ceiling.

The walls could not be papered immediately because of recent treatment against damp. The rope border design and the chintz 'Clandon Bell' are taken from wallpapers

in the Whitworth Art Gallery. The tablecloth and chair seats are in a seaweed design in two shade of blue and green on a sand ground, taken from a printed cotton in the Victoria and Albert Museum.

The dining room table is false, consisting of a circle of chipboard covered with a tablecloth. Around it are a set of carved mahogany chairs from about 1830. They are similar to designs by Whitaker of 1826-7 and T.King of 1829, in 'Modern Style Exemplified'.

The arrangement of the chimney-piece is again symmetrical, with a pair of bronze kneeling Egyptian figures c.1810, and a pair of gilt bronze neo-rococo English candlesticks in the French manner, from about 1830, flanking a bronze bust of Cicero, possibly by Francesco Righetti (1738-1819).

The combination of black and gold in the ornaments echoes the black and gold of the looking-glass frame. J.Kent, the architect, wrote in the 'Architectural Magazine' of 1835 about the decoration of a dining room that 'Bronze or brass ornaments on a black ground or wholly black are most appropriate.' Below, the brass fire irons are placed standing up vertically against the jamb of the fireplace, according to contemporary custom. On the other side of the fireplace is a pair of painted wooden 'Gothick' pedestals, very similar to the terminal newels of a staircase at Highclere, Hampshire, by James Barry of c.1860, but with a delicacy reminiscent of James Wyatt's Library at Lee Priory, Kent, of c.1783-90. Such was the persistence of the 'Strawbery Hill Gothick' first made popular by Horace Walpole in the 1750's.

All the pictures in this room, with one exception, are architectural studies. In the centre of the long wall is a water-colour of a 'Reconstruction of the Interior of the Temple of Athene Parthenos' possibly by Robert Smirke, (1781-1867) later the architect of the British Museum. It is drawn in the manner of J.M.Gandy (1771-1843), Sir John Soane's draughtsman, and includes the colossal figure of Athene Parthenos, which we know from classical descriptions to have been made in ivory and gold adorned with precious stones. Flanking this, and on the short walls to the right and left of the fireplace are four prints by the architect Giovanni Battista Piranesi from his volume *'Diverse maniere d'adornare i camini'* (*Various Ways of Decorating Chimney-pieces*). It includes designs other than for chimney-pieces, including furniture, sedan chairs, clocks and utensils. Piranesi, a friend of Robert Adam, championed classical Rome as opposed to classical

Greece in the dialectic of the time. He is best known for his *'Views of Rome'* and a series of fantastical prisons, *'I Carceri.'*

Below the Piranesis are a drawing by Sir Jeffry Wyatville (1766-1840) for fire-screens for Windsor Castle and a drawing from the architectural office of Charles Barry (1795-1860), for the Travellers Club, Pall Mall, (1829-31). It is in his Italian Renaissance manner. Immediately above the looking-glass is a coloured engraving of 1761 by Domenico Cunego after Gavin Hamilton (1723-1798), of 'Adromache's Farewell to Hector'. This Scot, who was working in Rome in the late 1750's and 60's, was one of the earliest exponents of the pure neo-classical style, taken up some fifteen years later by the French painter Jacques-Louis David (1748-1825).

The table is set for the dessert course at dinner. There is a charming description of the New Year's day dinner at Oakley Park, Shropshire, in 1852, written by Anna Maria Fay, in *'Victorian Days in England'*. She describes the dessert course: 'The dessert service was of pretty china, but nothing remarkable. The ices and jellies and other most beautifully arranged and delicious dishes were placed on the table. The dessert was composed of every variety of fruit, oranges, pears, grapes etc ..... Sitting a little while after dessert, Lady Harriet gave the signal to rise and we left the room ..... We entered the large and elegant drawing room. Coffee was brought in, and some ladies sat down to their beautiful Worcestered work, while others disposed themselves around the room .....'

On the table here we have an elaborate white lace tablecloth with a dessert service of hard paste porcelain, made in Paris c.1810, decorated in the neo-classical taste and richly gilded, by Nast of Rue des Amandiers, Popincourt (1783-1835). The flower arrangement of a bunch in a tall narrow-necked vase is according to the custom of the time.

Below: Mary Ellen Best. 'Dining Table at the home of Dr. Best' (1838).

THE · KITCHEN

This would have had a very different appearance with a cast iron range, a many shelfed painted dresser and a stoneware sink. Labour saving devices now happily take the place of kitchen maids. Modern pine kitchen cupboards have been fitted with the machines hidden behind them, so that no white plastic or formica is visible. The work tops were constructed from solid mahogany counters from a Victorian cotton warehouse in Manchester. The lower part of the walls have been clad with Laura Ashley cream tiles, and the decoration of sand painted walls finished with the blue rope border, has been extended from the dining room. The dark brown cooker, sink unit and dishwasher are recessive and tone with the mahogany work tops.

Kitchens today all too often resemble chemists' laboratories rather than congenial places for concocting delicious food. Here a compromise has been reached between the character of the antique and the convenience of the modern.

THE · TENT · ROOM OR · BOUDOIR

When the house was bought this small room on the mezzanine had been converted into a kitchen for the top floor flat. Because of its irregular shape, with a wide sloping chimney breast it was decided to 'tent' this room and make it into a boudoir. The design came from a drawing of 1800 for a tented alcove by Crace & Co., in the Cooper Hewitt Museum, New York. The idea of such tented rooms seems to have originated in France in the second half of the eighteenth century, but does not appear to have become fashionable in England until the nineteenth century. The Crace design used here is one of the earliest known English designs, while most surviving examples of tented rooms in England date only from the mid nineteenth century. To achieve this effect battening was attached to the ceiling along the flat walls, and across the alcoves. Loosely gathered material was then hung on curtain tracks attached to this, and the festoon pelmets stapled directly on to the wood above it. Behind the hangings, the uneven alcoves provide ample hanging space and bookshelves. In this way an elegant feature was created out of an oddly shaped room, and additional unobtrusive storage space provided. The fabric, in a design of multi-coloured stripes and flowers on a pale lemon ground, was taken from an eighteenth century hand painted silk in the Whitworth Art Gallery, Manchester. The linen fringe has been specially dyed crimson to link the colour in the flowers with the staircase beyond. The window curtains are held back by a pair of Victorian gilded copper curtain tie-backs, in the form of acanthus leaves. This room faces north, and the choice of pale yellow gives it an especially warm, sunny atmosphere.

The ottoman, scattered with cushions, in a rich 17th century Spanish faded crimson and yellow appliquéd silk, together with the pierced Egyptian brass stand, infuse the room with a flavour of Islam which would have appealed to the Victorians and their taste for exotica. The only other pieces of furniture are the Victorian black and gold lacquer chairs and an early nineteenth century mahogany bed table. This table is an ingenious device which has various screws and ratchets to raise the height and angle of the top for reading and writing in bed. At each of the four corners is a candle stand which can be swivelled out when needed, and remain level, even when the top is tilted. It has a single turned baluster leg at one end standing on a flat base on castors, which can be pushed under the bed, bringing the top over the bed to the required position. Here the table is used as a writing desk, with blotter, black lacquer pen tray and letter rack, and chamber sticks grouped around a glass dome of brightly coloured exotic birds. This room is lit by an eighteenth century Venetian lamp of gilded copper.

Left: 'A Tented Alcove' circa 1800. A design by Crace & Co.

THE · MAIN · BEDROOM

In Loudon's *'Encyclopaedia'* the anonymous contributor stated that for the bedrooms 'a light and cheerful style of colouring is most appropriate. A greater degree of contrast may here be admitted between the room and its furniture, than in any other apartment, as the bed curtains etc. form a sufficient mass to balance a tint of equal intensity upon the walls. There may also for the same reason be admitted gayer and brighter colours upon the carpet. The bed and window curtains should be of silk, woollen stuff, chintz, dimity or printed calico, according to the fortune or taste of the owner. Besides the bed, the furniture of the room consists of bed steps, containing a night stool and pot closet on each side of the bed ..... a few pictures or glazed prints upon the walls would add to the cheerful appearance of the room.'

The architect Mr. Kent wrote in Loudon's *'Architectural Magazine'* of 1835, that a bedchamber should be an 'airy, cheerful-looking apartment rather elegantly furnished, but in a plainer style than the living rooms. The walls look best when papered, the doors and windows painted to suit the paper. I should prefer a floor that could be washed, that is not a polished oak floor, and would not have the whole covered with carpet.'

Structurally the room has altered little, other than losing its fireplace. This was not replaced, as the long wall, which would originally have taken the bed, has been pierced to make an entrance into the room behind, allowing for an interconnecting bedroom and large bathroom.

This bedroom has two floor-length south facing windows. It has been given 'a light and cheerful colour' by using a yellow trompe l'oeil moiré paper, with a border of yellow roses and green scroll work, on a donkey grey ground. The curtains and bed hangings contrast with this and are in a grey trompe l'oeil moiré printed on satin cotton, which gives a very rich effect. The same border as on the walls has been used to edge the curtains.

The bed hangings have been lined with yellow moiré, and the bed cover is in the same material. The moiré is adapted from a nineteenth century design in the Whitworth Art Gallery, Manchester, and the border is a faithful copy of an example in the same collection.

The design for the canopy over the bed is adapted from a design 'Le Lit de Pied' in an undated, late nineteenth century French book called *'Le Petit Garde Meuble Collection de Sièges et Tentures'* published by Guilmard. At the foot of the bed there was usually placed a sofa or chaise longue. On this occasion a mahogany hall bench the design of which was taken from Thomas King, *'The Modern Style Exemplified ....'* (1839), has been substituted.

The room was decorated to take the fine mahogany bedroom suite consisting of a gentleman's clothes press, a chest of drawers and a looking-glass, all decorated with carved marine motifs, including dolphins, ropes and shells. The clothes press and chest of drawers were bought in S.E. London, not far from Greenwich. This may suggest they were specially made for a naval officer. The black Regency chairs with sabre legs, brass shells and beading, and rope work backs also echo the nautical flavour of the room. After the triumphs of the battles of the Nile and Trafalgar, marine ornament often appeared on Regency furniture.

Above: 'Le Lit de Pied' from 'Le Petit Garde Meuble' publ. by Guilmard.

The mahogany dressing table which is inlaid with ebony has a toilet mirror above. Beside the bed are mahogany bed steps, complete with night stool. The original chamber pot is secreted below the lift up top, and the treads of the steps are fitted with the original Brussels weave carpet. A cheval glass of c.1800 completes the furnishings.

The walls have been hung with 'glazed prints' which include a pair of French 18th century engravings by Avril-'La double Recompense du Merité', and 'Le Patriotisme Francais,' both dated 1788. Over the bed is a mezzotint after the Rev. Matthew William Peters (1742-1814), R.A., Chaplain to the Prince Regent, who was renowned for his paintings of deshabillé girls. The original of this, so the dedication on the print informs us, was in the Grosvenor collection. Above the looking-glass on the chest of drawers, and echoing its ovoid form, is a print by Angelica Kauffmann of 'Cupid and Euphrosyne'. An impression of this print was bought by William Duesbury's porcelain factory at Derby, which then reproduced the subject both as porcelain groups, and as painted vignettes.

The idea of scrubbed boards for a bedroom, as advocated by Loudon, seems a little spartan today, so a wood-brown fitted carpet has been substituted which continues through into the bathroom.

THE · MAIN
BATHROOM-DRESSING · ROOM

'No house of any pretensions will be devoid of a general bathroom, and in a large house there must be several of them. A good bathroom will always possess a wash basin ..... a water closet also ought to be in conjunction if possible or the plan of putting a seat in the bathroom itself may perhaps generally be adopted', wrote Robert Kerr in *'The Gentleman's House'*, 1865.

By making the bathroom interconnecting with the bedroom, it acts as a dressing room as well. Because of this the decorative scheme of yellow, grey and green has been continued throughout. The bath, which is copied from a Victorian cast iron original, is by C.P.Hart of London. With claw feet and brass taps and shower attachment, it stands in the middle of the room giving the bather a view down the street. The pair of oval, Victorian style wash basins are set in a marble top, and supported on a commode made from gothic pew doors from the demolished church of St. Luke's, Cheetham Hill, Manchester. Also in the Gothick taste is the large oak chair with pierced trefoil cresting and finials. A mahogany towel rail, and a mahogany hanging wardrobe complete the room.

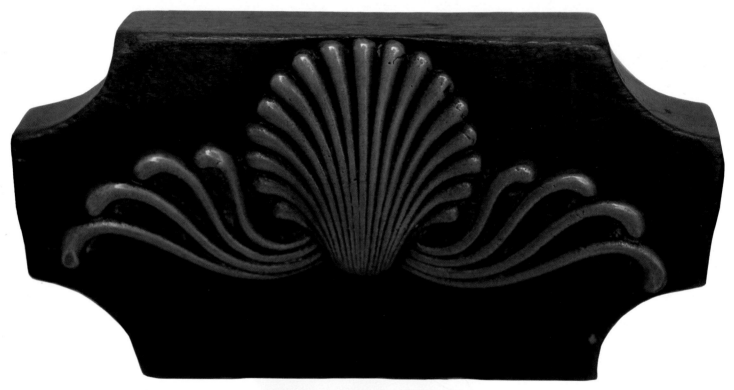

THE
FRENCH · BEDROOM

The Louis XV and XVI revival in the first half of the nineteenth century, often known as 'Old French' style, and propagated by the design books of Priestley and Weale, justifies the inclusion of the French room in this house. It was this revival of the French styles in fact that, William Morris later so strongly disliked.

The only structural alteration made to this room was to remove the unsightly cupboard from under the wash basin and replace it with a 'skirt' of material to match the curtains.

The pink, grey and white medallion design of the French curtains has been copied from a late eighteenth century French printed cotton in the Whitworth Art Gallery. The grey, white and pink striped wallpaper, inspired by prints of the period, has been edged with a border of bows and ribbons adapted from the material. The idea of the curtains running the whole length of the wall framing the bed comes from the French nineteenth century book of designs *Le Petit Garde Meuble Collection de Sièges et Tentures* published by Guilmard. It is called 'Alcove avec cabinets', as the curtains on either side of the bed conceal hanging space and shelves. This solves the problem of unsightly fitted cupboards, in a room too small to take a proper wardrobe. The bed is covered with a Victorian Paisley shawl of silk and cashmere, and strewn with linen and lace cushions of the same period.

Above: 'Alcove avec Cabinets'.
'Le Petit Garde Meuble'
published by Guilmard.

The dressing table is a rectangle of chipboard with a cover made from Laura Ashley lace panels. This form of dressing table was fashionable from the end of the eighteenth century throughout the nineteenth century. One of the earliest examples appears in Zoffany's (1734-1810) portrait of 'Queen Charlotte in her Dressing Room at Buckingham House', and they recur in water-colours of bedrooms until the end of the century. Standing on the dressing table are a pair of Louis XVI ormolu candlesticks, and some dishes in gilt and white porcelain made by Nast of Paris, circa 1810. A pair of Dutch eighteenth century walnut chairs in the French manner echo the medallion design of the material, both in the oval shape of the back and in the portrait medallion on the cresting. This portrait medallion is again repeated in the print, by St. Aubin, dated 1765, after the portrait by Cochin of the great French collector P.J.Mariette, which hangs over the bed.

Below: Queen Charlotte in her Dressing Room at Buckingham House by Zoffany. It shows the use of white lace on the dressing table.

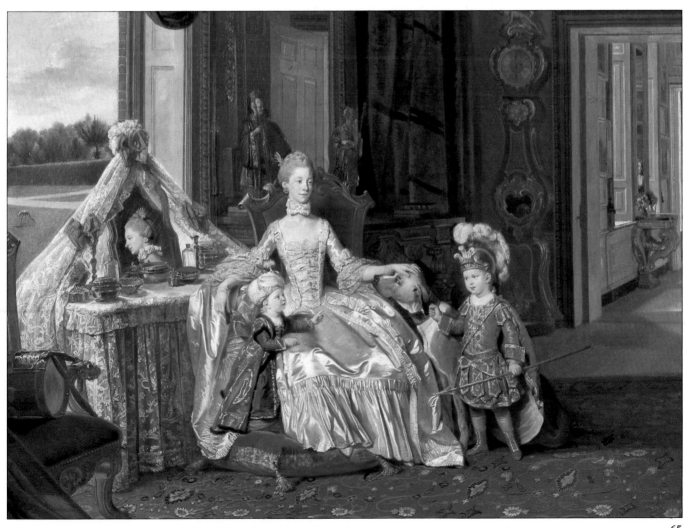

THE
BLUE · & · WHITE
BATHROOM

A water-colour of 1827 by Gerhardt Wilhelm von Reutern of his own bedroom, and C.P.Hart's reproduction of a Victorian bathroom suite transfer-printed with a design of flowers in blue on a white ground, were the starting point for this bathroom. Laura Ashley have printed a blue and white striped wallpaper which provides a good foil for the bathroom suite. Over the basin is a reproduction Victorian light with a glass shade. Victorian style Nottingham lace curtains have been used in front of plain sapphire blue curtains, instead of behind them. These are framed by a simple pelmet of a single swag, in a sprigged design, similar to the one in the water-colour. Chinese Kang Xsi porcelain of the 17th century stands on the white tiled shelf.

A Victorian mahogany towel rail and a white wicker chair lined in blue and white cotton are the only furniture in this room. White, sapphire and china blue towels pick out the colours of the wallpaper. On the walls hang a set of framed 18th century illustrated song sheets.

Below: Pelmet design from Thomas King's 'Upholsterer's Guide' of 1848.

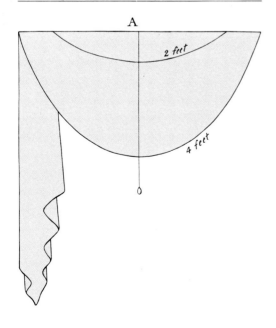

66

A modern reproduction of a Victorian lavatory, with underglaze blue transfer-printed decoration, supplied by C.P.Hart, and fitted with a mahogany seat.

Right: The matching wash-hand basin with underglaze blue transfer-printed decoration of garlands of flowers, brass taps and supported on cast-iron brackets copied from Victorian originals.

...esign from T.King's
...erer's Guide' of 1848.

THE · SWEET · PEA · BEDROOM

The only structural alteration that has been made here, was to remove the wash basin. The early nineteenth century chintz design of trailing sweet peas in sugar pink, burgundy, green, and aquamarine on a white ground was taken from a nineteenth century printed cotton in the Whitworth Art Gallery's collection. The type of pelmet and corner bed was copied from an early nineteenth century watercolour of 'A Bedroom' by Marcel Blairat, dated 1883. The 'lit de coin' also appears in a French upholsterers pattern book *'Le Petit Garde-Meuble'* published by Guilmard. It provides a simple and inexpensive way of dressing up a bed and occupies considerably less room than a four poster. Hanging space has been hidden behind a curtain. The design of the pelmet appears in Thomas King's *'Upholsterers Guide'* of 1848 . This sunny room has cool aquamarine walls in a small all-over textured design which picks out the pale green in the leaves. The burgundy border of the trompe-l'oeil twined braid, which is copied from a nineteenth century wallpaper border in the Whitworth Art Gallery, has been cut out along the scalloped edge, and echoes the darker shade of the sweet peas.

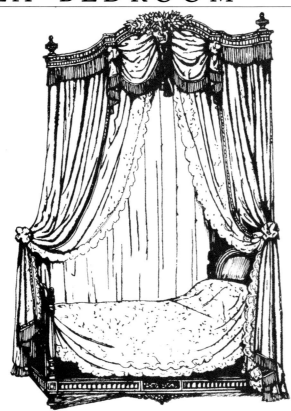

Above: 'Le lit de coin' from 'Le Petit Garde Meuble' published by Guilmard.

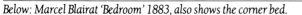

Below: Marcel Blairat 'Bedroom' 1883, also shows the corner bed.

All the furniture is early nineteenth century beech painted in shades of buff, blue, and green. It includes a wash stand, chest of drawers and set of chairs. These all have their original painted decoration. From the 1960's onwards much painted furniture was stripped, during the fashion for stripped pine. Mercifully, although rather late, many people are now preserving those pieces that still retain their original painted decoration, and some are even re-painting and stencilling those that have been stripped. The only piece of mahogany furniture in the room is an early Victorian button-backed chair covered in faded sea-green velvet. The dressing table is another simple rectangular table covered in material to match the curtains. On it stands a Regency burr walnut toilet mirror with three drawers and brass handles. In front of it is a green shagreen brush and mirror set, the aquamarine of which repeats that in the wallpaper and fabric. Shagreen or 'shark skin' was popular for small items like snuff boxes from the eighteenth century onwards. To the right is a heart-shaped, velvet covered Victorian jewel box, and a glass and ormolu watch case. The front opens and on the deep buttoned pink silk back there is a gilt hook on which to hang a ladies fob watch, thus keeping it safe overnight, and making a useful bedside clock.

The pottery which is mostly 18th and 19th century English, includes a Wedgwood plate decorated in a design of sea-green seaweed and shells, a Bristol hard paste porcelain bowl decorated in swags of flowers in green, and a mauve and white Staffordshire jug and basin inscribed with the name of the owner, Jane Birkin. The cupid motif suggests that this may have been a wedding present. On the walls are a series of nineteenth century 'glazed prints' of Hawking after Samuel Howitt (1742-1841), and some plates from a book on butterflies. Above the chest of drawers is a print of a 'Victorian Wedding in Sherborne Abbey', flanked by a Bartolozzi stipple engraving after Richard Cosway of 'Madame Récamier', Napoleon's mistress, and a black chalk drawing of an unknown woman by Gainsborough Dupont (1754-1797), the nephew of Thomas Gainsborough (1727-1788). In the bed alcove is an engraving of 'The Apotheosis of Charlotte Augusta of Wales', the daughter of George IV, who died in childbirth in 1818. It is inscribed 'To perpetuate the memory of this amiable princess so justly beloved and regretted by the British nation.' Above the wash stand is a framed piece of unfinished embroidery dating from 1700. The design of the whole composition has been drawn in black ink on ivory satin, but only the lower portion has been embroidered, in coloured silk. It was intended, when finished, to have been made up into a toilet mirror with eight drawers beneath, similar in format to the one on the dressing table. In the semi-circular headed frame is the Old Testament scene of 'King Solomon and the Queen of Sheba', and supporting it at the bottom are the Lion and Unicorn of England. The rest is made up of flowers and fruit. On the brown carpeted floor is a mid nineteenth century needlework rug.

THE · GARDEN

The only evidence that survives to show how the garden originally looked is the 1868 street map, which shows a dotted oval in the centre of the plot, and various trees or shrubs. The restorers task was how to interpret this. When the house was bought the garden had been completely tarmacadamed. For practical reasons it was decided to keep a parking space for one car at the far end, but rather than fence it off altogether, this has been divided from the main garden by a rustic arbour à la Humphrey Repton (1752-1818). This was built out of thin tree trunks complete with bark and irregularities, to provide a climbing frame for roses and vines. In this way a virtue was made of a necessity, and the space can double up as parking or a shady arbour. As the garden faces north and the trees would have created more shade it was decided to pave the central area rather than turf it, and limit greenery to the flower beds and climbing plants on the walls. The paved area has been made from bricks radiating outwards in a circular design. The oval shape had to be abandoned because of the reduced space. A few bricks have been removed and the gaps planted with sweet smelling herbs, like cammomile and thyme, that scent the garden when trodden on.

J.C. Loudon, whose 'Encyclopaedia of Cottage, Farm and Villa Architecture' has been extensively quoted, was one of the leading exponents of the 'Gardenesque' style, and published various books on garden planning including 'The Suburban Gardener and Villa Companion' in 1836. Derek Clifford in his 'A History of Garden Design' writes 'Loudon, the high priest of the gardenesque style or lack of it, was surprisingly the very man to put his finger on the essential change of outlook between the eighteenth and nineteenth centuries. He pointed out that the stream of books on the aesthetics of gardening had narrowed to a trickle, dried up and been replaced by a flood of gardening literature which was almost solely concerned to introduce new varieties of plants to its readers and to instruct them how they should be grown.' The garden of this house has been planted with as wide a variety of shrubs and plants as the space allowed and which would have been used in a garden of this date. Garden planning had been taken out of the hands of the architects and designers and taken over by gardeners whose main interest was growing plants, particularly of the more exotic nature that had recently been introduced from abroad, like cammelias and magnolias. Planting was planned to achieve colour throughout the year, against a background of evergreen, to give substance to the garden even in winter. The use of bedding plants to give additional colour also became popular at this time, owing to the widespread use of greenhouses to bring plants on.

The table and chairs are modern cast iron copies of Victorian originals. They have been painted dark green as they would have been in the 19th century. The present day taste for white would make them the focal point of the garden rather than allowing the emphasis to be on the rustic arbour, the plants and the sculpture.

The 18th century German stone garden ornament represents a giant's mask with trailing hollyhocks in his hair, being tweaked by an impudent young faun.

THE · TRANSFORMATION · OF · A · HOUSE

ENTRANCE · HALL

STAIRCASE

DRAWING ROOM

DETAIL · OF CORNICE

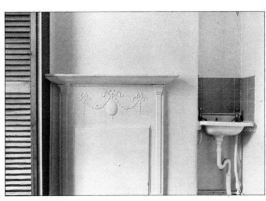

DINING · ROOM

KITCHEN

KITCHEN

TENT · ROOM
OR · BOUDOIR

MAIN
BEDROOM

MAIN
BEDROOM

MAIN
BATHROOM

FRENCH
BEDROOM

BLUE · & · WHITE BATHROOM

SWEET · PEA BEDROOM

ACKNOWLEDGEMENTS

THE AUTHOR WOULD LIKE TO THANK THE FOLLOWING PEOPLE FOR THEIR ASSISTANCE IN THE PREPARATION OF THIS BOOK:

Richard Gray, James Lomax, Thom Richardson of the **Decorative Arts Department, Manchester City Art Galleries**. Frances Collard, of the **Furniture and Woodwork Department, Victoria and Albert Museum** who kindly made available her unpublished material on 19th century upholstery. **The Costume & Textile Department of the Victoria and Albert Museum**. Michael Clarke, Dr Jennifer Harris and Maude Wallace of the **Whitworth Art Gallery**, Manchester. P.A.Bezodis, of the **Survey of London** who made available unpublished material on the locality. **Diana Chalmers** for organising the building work. Lastly I would like to thank my husband Tim for his help and support throughout all stages of the book.

LAURA ASHLEY WOULD LIKE TO THANK THE FOLLOWING PHOTOGRAPHIC CREDITS:

HISTORY · OF · THE · HOUSE	P.4 & 5	Maps of Kensington and Post Card c.1900, Royal Borough of Kensington & Chelsea Local History Library.
DRAWING · ROOM	P.12	'Drawing Room at Chester Place' - Clarendon Gallery.
	P.17	Gillow Drawing - Westminster Public Library.
	P.24	Joseph William Margetts 'Corner of a Sitting Room' - Hazlitt, Gooden & Fox.
	P.26	'Louisa Paris Drawing Room in Dover Street' - Hazlitt, Gooden & Fox.
	P.26/27	Mary Ellen Best 'General Norcliffe in his Study at Langton Hall' - Sotheby's.
MORNING · ROOM	P.33	Pelmet from Thomas King's 'Upholsterer's Guide' - Victoria & Albert Museum Library.
DINING · ROOM / KITCHEN	P.41	Mary Ellen Best 'Dr Best's Dining Table' - Sotheby's.
TENT · ROOM · OR · BOUDOIR	P.47	Crace & Co. 'A Tented Alcove' c.1800 - Cooper Hewitt Museum, New York.
FRENCH · BEDROOM	P.65	Zoffany - 'Queen Charlotte in her Dressing Room at Buckingham House' reproduced by Gracious Permission of Her Majesty the Queen.
BLUE · & · WHITE · BATHROOM	P.66	Pelmet from Thomas King's 'Upholsterer's Guide' - Victoria & Albert Museum Library.
	P.68/69	Gerhardt Wilhelm von Reutern 'The Artist's Room' - Hazlitt, Gooden & Fox.
SWEET · PEA · BEDROOM	P.72	Marcel Blairat 'Bedroom' - Hazlitt, Gooden & Fox.
	P.74/75	Pelmet from Thomas King's 'Upholsterer's Guide' - Victoria & Albert Museum Library.

LAURA ASHLEY WOULD LIKE TO THANK THE FOLLOWING PEOPLE FOR WORKS CARRIED OUT:

Dry Rot and Damp Treatment: **Rentokil**. Plumber: **Priority Plumbing**. Builder: **Dennis & Co.**, St. Albans. Drawing Room plaster frieze and roses: **J.D.McDonough**, 347 New Kings Road, Fulham, London. Reproduction light fittings: **Christopher Wray** (Hall), **Peter Jones** (Bathrooms). Old brass door handles: **Christopher Wray**. Old brass door plates: **Camden Passage**. Carpets: Drawing Room, **Laura Ashley Decorator Collection**. Plain Carpets: **D.B.Carpets**, Workingham, Surrey. Kitchen Units: **Homecharm Furniture Ltd**. P.O.Box 3, Manchester Old Road, Middleton, Manchester. Reproduction Bathroom fittings: **C.P.Hart & Sons**, Hercules Road, London. Kitchen electrical equipment by **Neff**. Garden Design: **Jamie Garnock**, 28 Tredgold Street, London. Garden Furniture: **Garden Crafts**, 158 New Kings Road, Fulham. Styling for photography: **Sasha de Stroumillo & Jane Clifford**.

LAURA ASHLEY WOULD LIKE TO THANK THE FOLLOWING COMPANIES FOR THE LOAN OF PRODUCTS:

DRAWING · ROOM	Assorted antique tapestry cushions from the 16th century from Heraz, 25 Motcomb Street, London SW1X 8JY. Tel 01 245 9497
	All books are large leather-bound volumes from Christopher Hodsoll, 69 Pimlico Road, London SW1W 8PH. Tel 01 730 2514 or 7454
TENT · ROOM · OR · BOUDOIR	Nineteenth century needlework rug from Heraz, 25 Motcomb Street, London SW1X 8JN. Tel 01 245 9497
MAIN · BEDROOM	Fragrance for the Discerning Gentleman from the Trumpers Collection Geo.F.Trumper, 9 Curzon St., London W1Y 7FL. Tel 01 499 1850
FRENCH · BEDROOM	White lace cushions from a selection at Lunn Antiques, 86 New Kings Road, Parsons Green, London SW6 4LU. Tel 01 730 4638
SWEET · PEA · BEDROOM	Nineteenth century needlework cushions from Heraz, 25 Motcomb Street, London SW1X 8JN. Tel 01 245 9497
	Nineteenth century needlework rug from Christopher Hodsoll, 69 Pimlico Road, London SW1W 8PH. Tel 01 730 2514 or 7454

LAURA ASHLEY WALLPAPERS AND MATERIALS USED IN THIS BOOK:

HALL	Wallpaper & material: Mr Jones F381. Border F274. Paint Navy, Sand & Burgundy.
DRAWING · ROOM	Laura Ashley Decorator Collection. Tudor Rose Sateen F362. Wallpaper border F265. Tudor Lattice Sateen P789, chair covers.
MORNING · ROOM	White Bower Chintz F364. Dark green Nutmeg edging. Border F391.
DINING · ROOM	Decorator Collection. Clarendon Bell F253. Seaweed F356. Paint Sand. Rope border F291.
MAIN · BEDROOM	Decorator Collection. Grey Moiré F301. Yellow Moiré F301. Yellow Moiré wallpaper.
FRENCH · BEDROOM	Medallion Sateen F255. Striped wallpaper F319. Wallpaper border F267.
BLUE · & · WHITE · BATHROOM	Cricket Stripe wallpaper F369. Curtains plain Sapphire with Nottingham lace panels. Pelmet Bembridge F66.
SWEET · PEA · BEDROOM	Decorator Collection. Wallpaper F256. Chintz F256. Rope border F336.

SELECTIVE BIBLIOGRAPHY:

John Cornforth: English Interior Decoration 1790-1840. The Quest for Comfort (1978). **Anna Maria Fay**: Victorian Days in England. **Guilmard** (publ.): Le Petit Garde Meuble undated. **Thomas Hope**: Household Furniture and Interior Decoration (1807). **Walter Houghton**: The Victorian Frame of Mind 1830-1870. **Owen Jones**: Grammar of Ornament (1856). **Robert Kerr**: The Gentleman's House or How to plan English Residences from the Parsonage to the Palace (1868). **Thomas King**: Upholsterer's Guide (1848). **Susan Lasden**: Victorians at Home (1981). **J.C.Loudon**: Encyclopaedia of Cottage Farm and Villa Architecture. First printed 1833, but reprinted several times by his widow (1867). Architectural Magazine (1835). Suburban Gardener and Villa Companion. **Nicolette Scourse**: The Victorians and their Flowers (1983). **Peter Thornton**: Authentic Décor. The Domestic Interior 1620-1920 (1984). Pictorial Dictionary of British 19th Century Furniture Designs.

Book Design and Artwork by the Laura Ashley Studio, Carno, Powys, Wales.